MINDSET ZONE

Actualize Your Human Potential

Ana Melikian, Ph.D.

Mindset Zone: Actualize Your Human Potential

Copyright © 2024 Ana Melikian, Ph.D.

AMAZE Press Zone Books

All rights reserved. No part of this book may be reproduced, scanned, or distributed in any manner whatsoever without written permission from the publisher or author, except in the case of brief quotations embodied in critical articles and reviews. For information, please contact: support@amazecoaching.com

Jones Media Publishing
10645 N. Tatum Blvd. Ste. 200-166
Phoenix, AZ 85028
JonesMediaPublishing.com

AMAZE Press Zone books are available at special discounts for bulk purchases by corporations, institutions, and other organizations. For information, please support@amazecoaching.com

Printed in the United States of America

ISBN: 979-8-9901930-0-0 paperback
12 11 10 9 8 7 6 5 4 3 2 1

Table of Contents

What You Need to Know vii

PART I: DEFINING MINDSETS 1

  1. What's a Mindset? 3

      Three Mindset Approaches 4

  2. Beliefs 5

      Fixed and Growth Mindsets 5

      The Complexity of Growth 7

      Personal Success Equation 8

      The Role of Praise and Effort 8

      Practical Applications 10

  3. Information-Processing Sets 15

      Deliberative vs. Implemental Mindsets 15

      The Role of Focus and Unfocus 16

      Understanding Procrastination 16

      Practical Applications Using WOOP 17

      WOOP in Action 19

4. Frames of Reference 25
   Global Mindsets in Leadership 25
   The Human Side of the AI Disruption 26
   Framework for Human Potential 28

5. Mindset Zone 35
   Mindset or Mindsets 35
   Practical Definition 36
   Accelerating Change........................37
   The Concept of the Mindset Zone...........39
   Navigating the Mindset Zone.............. 40

PART II: ACTUALIZE YOUR POTENTIAL..........45

6. Mindset Limitations - Side A 49
   Visual Blind Spots........................... 49
   Mindset blind spots......................... 51
   Heroes and Sheroes.........................53
   Learning Journey 54
   Life Circumstances..........................57

7. Mindset Limitations – Side B 63
   The Influence of Thought on Action 63
   Cognitive Behavioral Therapy (CBT)........ 64
   Beyond Linear Change 66
   Insights Are Not Enough ....CG
   The Power of Just Exhaling 68

Visualizing Change: The Triangle Model 68

   Expand What's Possible. .70

8. The P.I.E. Method. 75

   The P.I.E. Method. 76

   "P" for Pause 76

   "I" for Increasing Self-Awareness 79

   "E" for Embracing Experimentation 81

9. Mindset Zone to Actualize Your Potential . . .87

   The Power of Mental Fitness 87

   A Safe Space for Growth 88

   The Journey of Continuous Learning 88

   Embracing the Flow of Optimal
       Performance 88

   Expand What's Possible! .89

PART III: RESOURCES 91

Notes 93

Acknowledgements 97

Thank you for reading! 101

Free GIFTS for YOU! 103

About the Author 105

What You Need to Know

Imagine. You are a pencil. Yes, a pencil. A wood cylinder with a carbon mine inside. What can you do as a pencil? Well, write, draw, sketch, doodle, annotate, and even write in space with zero gravity! When you pause to think about it, you're amazing!

Imagine. You rarely sharpen your pencil. A pencil with a worn tip is difficult to use, and the results you get are not as sharp and effective as they could be. You know this.

Why don't you stop and sharpen your pencil?

No time. Too many things going on. No sharpener at hand.

Add your own excuse to this list.

Whatever your excuse may be, whether you want to admit it or not, you're not tapping into your full potential.

You could choose to press the pause button, be aware of yourself, discover your thinking patterns, name your feelings and emotions, and see your actions and behaviors under a different light. You might even see your amazing potential in your mind's eye first. And that is the goal here, to empower you to press the pause button, increase your self-awareness, and experiment with something new.

Yes. The goal here is to offer you a safe space where you can sharpen your pencil.

You have the power to transform the life you have now into the life you dream of, desire, and deserve.

Mindset work can be one of the best tools to "sharpen your pencil," but sometimes, it can also get you frustrated. Maybe you consume more than your fair share of self-development materials and still struggle to implement what you learn in your daily life. Others seem to have found a way to break out, achieving more while enjoying the process and creating an impact while having a life, too. You've even had glimpses of this in your own life, but it isn't your MO - Modus Operandi. These moments of hope and delight prove it's possible, yet they often remain elusive.

To change this dynamic, it's important to understand what mindsets are, how they work, and how they create the life you're living.

Once you learn how to work with your mindsets, you can leverage your strengths, compensate for your weaknesses, and be well on your way to living the life you've been dreaming about for so long.

Let's dive in!

PART I

DEFINING MINDSETS

1.
What's a Mindset?

In my work with clients, I have discovered two almost universal gaps in the core understanding of what mindsets really are.

First, there isn't just one way to define mindset. In fact, there are nearly as many definitions of mindset as there are mindset experts – that's the bad news.

Second, most of these definitions can be quickly and easily categorized into three different approaches[1] – that's the good news.

Understanding each of these specific perspectives can clear away the clutter when you Google the word "mindset" and find yourself staring at over 600 million results or when you search Amazon and find the term "mindset" showing up in more than 30,000 books, or even when you discover over 3,300 podcasts with the word "mindset" in the title.

Now, with the advent of so many AI tools for content generation, these numbers will get outdated quickly.

Three Mindset Approaches

Probably, the most well-known one, popularized by positive psychology, is seeing mindsets as beliefs.

Another, based on cognitive psychology research, focuses on information-processing styles used to master different types of tasks.

Finally, organizational leadership experts tend to see mindsets as predispositions that inform our worldviews, that is, as filters through which we look at the world.

Let's look into these three approaches and how they can change your life.

2.
Beliefs

Like many others in positive psychology, Dr. Carol Dweck, a Professor of Psychology at Stanford University, sees mindsets as the beliefs we hold about our human potential for learning and change[1]. In her book, *Mindset: The New Psychology of Success*, Dr. Dweck speaks about fixed and growth mindsets[2].

Fixed and Growth Mindsets

Consider an ability you don't think you're particularly good at. For me, it's singing. It's difficult to believe I can ever be a good enough singer to perform in front of an audience. In essence, I have a fixed mindset around my singing. My self-perception about singing is to believe that I wasn't lucky enough to be born with that innate talent, so I must resign and accept the "facts" of nature.

Can you identify an ability you see yourself lacking the talent to be good at? If so, then you have identified one of your many fixed mindsets.

On the other hand, we have a growth mindset when we hold the belief that through dedication and hard work, we can develop our talents and skills within a specific area.

Me? I wasn't very good at school to the point I almost failed 4th grade because of my bad spelling due to undiagnosed dyslexia. Yet I held the belief that I had what I needed to make it if I worked hard enough. I was open to learning, which made me more resilient, and I exceeded my expectations, ending high school as one of the top students. In hindsight, dyslexia became my superpower.

Having to work sometimes twice as hard to achieve the same results as some of my peers helped me develop grit. Plus, I could positively channel my stubbornness. Now I understand that more than a learning disorder, dyslexia is a different way of processing information[3] that can have significant advantages. In my particular case, it helps me excel in pattern detection and problem-solving.

The Complexity of Growth

Dr. Dweck's research underscores that our beliefs about our abilities significantly influence our approach to learning and growth. However, it's crucial to recognize that adopting a growth mindset doesn't guarantee professional success in every endeavor.

Going back to my example about singing, I could embrace a growth mindset and put effort into developing my singing capabilities, and I could learn to hold a tune and sing in front of an audience. But this doesn't imply that it's merely a question of willpower for me to become a professional singer. The reality is more complex than that. Yes, there are many examples of singers who achieved incredible accolades and were criticized for not having the best vocal capacities. Likewise, there are plenty of extraordinary backup singers with vocal talent that can bring the house down, yet they never made it to stardom.

Personal growth and success are not linear journeys defined by sheer willpower or innate talent alone. They are intricate processes influenced by a myriad of factors, including effort, strategy, persistence, and circumstances beyond our control.

Personal Success Equation

In *Three Feet from Gold*[4], Sharon L. Lechter and Greg S. Reid articulate what they called "Your Success Equation" as:

$$((P + T) \times A \times A) + F = \text{Your Success Equation}$$

Add P for Passion (something that makes your heart sing) to T for Talent (something you excel in.) Then multiply it (P+T) by the right Associations, first A (people or organizations that can support you) and Actions, second A (concrete steps you can take toward your goal.) Last but not least, add to all these ((P + T) x A x A) the unwavering belief in yourself, represented by F for Faith, and you have your unique success equation.

If you embrace a growth mindset while actualizing your success equation, you open yourself to even more possibilities.

The Role of Praise and Effort

Also, take into account that praising a talent or ability can inadvertently foster a fixed mindset, leading individuals to avoid challenges and fear failure.

Consider a child who excels in math effortlessly, earning him a place in an advanced class. His teachers praise him for his math abilities, and his parents brag about having a son in advanced math. He believes he is really smart and feels very proud of it. However, as the material becomes more challenging, he doesn't get the concepts immediately, and he starts getting "B"s, instead of "A⁺"s. He starts to doubt himself— maybe he isn't as smart as he thought. His self-esteem takes a hit, eventually leading him to avoid math. This scenario illustrates how a fixed mindset, when confronted with difficulty, can undermine confidence and motivation.

In contrast, praising the process—effort, strategy, and perseverance—encourages a growth mindset, fostering resilience and a love for learning. This small but important shift can help you see challenges as opportunities for growth rather than threats to your self-esteem and identity. Moreover, this can lead to the belief of "You can do this if you work hard," even leading to grit becoming part of your identity.

Practical Applications

To cultivate a growth mindset, we can start by rephrasing our self-talk and the feedback we give to others. Instead of saying "I cannot do this," add "yet" — "I cannot do this, yet." Adding this simple word implies that improvement is possible and within reach.

The journey from a fixed to a growth mindset is transformative. It's about embracing the power of belief to shape our learning and resilience and, ultimately, our identity and lives. By understanding the role of effort, the impact of praise, and the potential of YET[5], we can unlock our potential and foster an environment that celebrates learning and growth.

Press PAUSE & Sharpen Your Pencil

Create a moment to increase your self-awareness, explore your thinking patterns, name your feelings and emotions, and see your actions and behaviors under a different light.

Increase Your Self-Awareness:

1. Reflect on a recent situation where you felt stuck or challenged. What were your initial thoughts and feelings about this situation?

2. Identify which mindset (fixed or growth) dominated your reaction. Did you see the challenge as a threat to your abilities or as an opportunity to learn?

3. Consider alternative ways you could have approached the situation with a growth mindset. How might this have changed your feelings and actions?

Embrace Experimentation:

Incorporate the power of "yet" into your daily life to transform how you face challenges and perceive your abilities.

This week, focus on an area where you've previously felt limited or encountered obstacles. Each time you catch yourself thinking, "I cannot do this," add "yet" to the end of that statement. For example:

- If you're struggling with learning a new skill, instead of saying, "I cannot understand this," tell yourself, "I cannot understand this, yet."
- When faced with a complex problem at work or school, instead of concluding, "I can't solve this," remind yourself, "I haven't solved this yet."

Create a "Power of Yet" journal. Each day, note down at least one instance where you applied the concept of "yet" to a challenge. Reflect on the following:

- How did adding "yet" change your emotional response to the situation?
- Did it alter your approach to overcoming the obstacle? How?
- Record any progress or insights gained from this shift in perspective.

This exercise is designed to help you internalize the growth mindset by recognizing that skills and abilities can be developed with time and effort. The word "yet" serves as a simple but powerful reminder that you are on a journey of continuous learning and growth.

3.
Information-Processing Sets

Cognitive psychologists have contributed significantly to our understanding of mindsets by framing them as information-processing sets—skills our brains use to master various tasks and challenges. This perspective illuminates the intricate processes behind our decision-making, goal-setting, and the execution of tasks, highlighting the adaptability and flexibility of the human mind.

Deliberative vs. Implemental Mindsets

A key distinction in this area of research is between deliberative and implemental mindsets[1]. When we're in a deliberative mindset, we're open-minded, weighing our options and considering the best course of action. This stage is crucial for setting meaningful, achievable goals based on a realistic assessment of our situation and preferences.

Conversely, once a decision is made, the implemental mindset takes over. This shift in thinking focuses on planning, execution, and overcoming obstacles. It's about turning our intentions into action through persistence, strategy, and adaptation to changing circumstances.

The Role of Focus and Unfocus

Interestingly, the value of being unfocused or allowing our minds to wander is often underestimated in the goal-setting process. While focus is undoubtedly vital for achieving our objectives, periods of unfocused thought can foster creativity, problem-solving, and the generation of new ideas. This rhythmic balance between focus and unfocus is essential for innovative thinking and effective decision-making.

Understanding Procrastination

This framework also offers insights into procrastination, a common challenge many of us face. Procrastination often arises not from laziness but from a lack of clear goals or commitment to a specific outcome. Without a clear destination and a realistic plan to get there, taking action can feel overwhelming or futile.

When I catch myself procrastinating, especially on tasks like responding to important emails, I pause to clarify my desired outcome and the steps needed to achieve it. This moment of pause and self-awareness can shift my mindset from indecision to purposeful action, illustrating the power of understanding and leveraging our information-processing sets.

Practical Applications Using WOOP

Understanding and applying the concepts of deliberative and implemental mindsets can significantly enhance our ability to set and achieve goals. The WOOP method[2], developed by psychologist and researcher Gabriele Oettingen, provides a powerful framework for this process, incorporating both mindsets in a structured manner:

1. **Wish**: Begin with a clear, achievable goal. Use the deliberative mindset to identify something you genuinely want to accomplish. This wish should be

challenging yet realistic, aligning with your deeper values and aspirations.

2. **Outcome**: Envision the best possible outcome that would result from fulfilling your wish. Imagine how you would feel and the impact it would have on your life. This visualization process taps into the motivational energy needed to pursue your goal, highlighting the benefits of achieving it.

3. **Obstacle**: Identify the internal obstacles that stand in the way of achieving your wish. These could be habits, fears, or beliefs that have previously hindered your progress. Recognizing these obstacles is crucial for preparing to overcome them, embodying a critical aspect of the implemental mindset.

4. **Plan**: Develop a plan to overcome your identified obstacles. This involves creating if-then statements (e.g., "If I encounter [obstacle], then I will [specific action to overcome or mitigate the obstacle]"). This step transforms the deliberation into actionable strategies, ensuring that you're prepared to face challenges head-on.

WOOP in Action

Let's apply the WOOP method to a common scenario: You wish to improve your physical fitness (Wish). The best outcome would be feeling healthier, more energetic, and confident in your physical abilities (Outcome). However, you recognize that a lack of time and motivation in the evenings are significant obstacles (Obstacle). To overcome this, you plan to schedule morning workout sessions three times a week and prepare your workout clothes the night before (Plan).

This approach not only clarifies what you want to achieve and why but also prepares you for the inevitable challenges, ensuring that your implemental mindset is equipped with concrete strategies for action.

The WOOP method exemplifies how a deep understanding of our cognitive processes and mindsets can be applied to personal development and goal achievement. By integrating deliberative and implemental mindsets with structured planning and reflection, we can navigate the complexities of behavior change and personal growth more effectively.

Press PAUSE & Sharpen Your Pencil

Reflect on how you process information, recognize your emotions, and observe your actions. This pause is an opportunity to illuminate your thought patterns and behaviors from a new perspective, enhancing your understanding of yourself and your interactions with the world around you.

Increase Your Self-Awareness:

Reflect on your decision-making process in a recent significant choice you faced. This could be related to your career, work, personal life, or any other area where you had to make a choice:

1. Identify the stage where you spent most of your time: Was it in deliberating the options (deliberative mindset) or planning and executing your decision (implemental mindset)?

2. Consider how your mindset during this process influenced the outcome. Did you feel prepared and confident

in your actions, or did you encounter unexpected challenges?

3. Think about the emotions and thoughts that arose during the decision-making process. How did they align with the mindset you were in?

Embrace Experimentation:

For the upcoming week, select a goal or decision you've been postponing or feeling uncertain about. Apply the WOOP method as a structured approach to tackle it, integrating both deliberative and implemental mindsets:

W. Wish: Clearly define what you wish to achieve or decide upon.

O. Outcome: Visualize the best possible outcome of achieving your wish. How would it feel? What impact would it have on your life?

O. Obstacle: Identify potential internal obstacles that could hinder your progress. These could be related to your mindset, emotions, or thought patterns.

P. Plan: Develop a concrete plan to overcome these obstacles. Create if-then action plans (e.g., "If I start to doubt my ability to complete this task, then I will remind myself of a past success where I overcame similar doubts").

Journaling Prompts:

Throughout the week, keep a journal of your experiences using this method. Reflect on the following:

- How did structuring your approach with WOOP influence your decision-making process?
- How did the WOOP method help you avoid procrastination?
- Document any progress towards your goal or decision, including how you navigated obstacles with your action plan.

These exercises aim to enhance your ability to navigate between different mindsets effectively, applying a structured approach to goal setting and problem-solving. By consciously moving between deliberative and implemental mindsets, you can gain deeper insights into your cognitive processes and how they influence your actions and outcomes.

4.
Frames of Reference

From another vantage point, organizational leadership experts place the spotlight on the cognitive filters individuals and communities use to see the world around them. Mindsets, in this case, work as frames of reference and can act as mental shortcuts, guiding our interpretations and responses to various situations.

Global Mindsets in Leadership

A critical aspect of modern leadership is the development of global mindsets. This necessity becomes evident when leading multinational teams, where success hinges on maintaining a worldwide business orientation while adapting to local cultures and environments.

A recent global roundtable hosted by the ACEC, the Association of Corporate Executive Coaches[1], illustrates this point well. A complex scenario was presented by a participant who spearheaded the implementation of a global performance management system within an international manufacturing firm. The initiative's key learnings highlighted the need for cultural adjustments, particularly in countries like China, where even at a manager-director level, they avoid standing out. In the European Union, privacy regulations regarding performance data, which are much tighter than in the US and Canada, necessitated careful navigation. Not surprisingly, fostering relationships with local managers emerged as a critical factor for grasping and respecting cultural nuances, ensuring the system's effectiveness across diverse regions.

The Human Side of the AI Disruption

Another example is the frame of reference I use to unlock human potential, a mission increasingly pertinent during the AI disruption.

We find ourselves at a crossroads in a world increasingly shaped by artificial intelligence

(AI). AI has been infiltrating our daily lives for some time now, from the personalized playlists of Spotify to the eerily accurate suggestions of Netflix and YouTube. The release of tools like Chat GPT introduced generative AI to the public and opened Pandora's box. Now, we see how AI can create content and ideas at lightning speed, including conversations, stories, images, videos, and music, blurring the lines between human creativity and machine-generated content.

This accelerating change is disrupting the life and work of many, bringing a mix of awe and anxiety and inevitably increasing the risks of burnout—how can we keep this pace? To add to the fire, we worry about deep fakes, job displacement, and even existential threats. Indeed, half of AI researchers acknowledge a tangible risk of human extinction if we don't build some guardrails for AI; the question looms large: Are we on the brink of a future once only imagined in science fiction?

The reality is stark—we cannot halt the tide of AI, yet this inevitability does not render us powerless. History has shown us, through the dual-edged sword of nuclear technology, that humanity can navigate the perils of its own ingenuity—we are still here! The key lies not in resistance but in response. How do we harness the transformative power of AI to enrich our lives without succumbing to its pitfalls?

Framework for Human Potential

By embracing, as our frame of reference, a holistic view of human potential, on the one hand, we can acknowledge that many of the problems we face are made worse by individual or people factors—and this dynamic is aggravated in uncertain times. On the other hand, we can recognize that the same individuals have untapped resources. We can release their potential through self-development work, learning from positive psychology, neuropsychology, behavioral, cognitive, and performance sciences. This inner work is foundational to unleashing the capabilities we all have as human beings and can help us navigate the accelerating change, we are living. Furthermore, it can help us see beyond our fears and uncertainties and explore the vast potential for positive change in AI.

Equally important is recognizing that we are connecting beings, too. If we learn to tap into the power of connections, groups, and communities, we can amplify our potential in significant ways. We can learn from each other, and together, we can preserve our humanity and shape a future that reflects our deepest values and aspirations.

Furthermore, the systems where we interact and live, with all their complexities, systemic rules, and diversity, can help us unlock the exponential power we might not know we have.

Accessing the potential of these different dimensions—inner, outer, and systems—allows us to transform problems into solutions and innovation.

This holistic approach expands what's possible in a big way. It's possible to harness the power of AI to augment human potential, ensuring that technological advancements enhance, rather than diminish, our humanity and well-being.

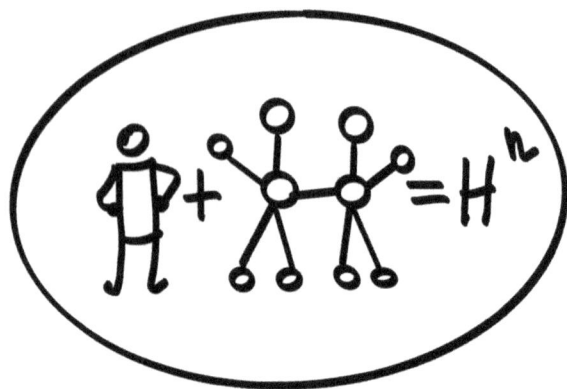

Figure 1: Frame of Reference to Unlock Human Potential. Let's consider the systems within which we live (represented by the ellipse in the image). In addition to self-development (represented by the stick figure), we leverage the power of community (represented by the connecting dots). We can unlock our human potential exponentially (represented by H^n).

Press PAUSE & Sharpen Your Pencil

As we explore the concept of frames of reference, it's essential to pause and reflect on how our own cognitive filters shape our perceptions and interactions with the world. This exercise is designed to increase your self-awareness and encourage you to experiment with new perspectives.

Increase Your Self-Awareness:

1. Reflect on Your Global Mindset: Think about a recent interaction or decision that involved cultural differences. How did your own cultural frame of reference influence your approach? Were there assumptions or biases that you recognized in retrospect?

2. Consider AI's Impact: Reflect on how artificial intelligence has already influenced your personal or professional life. What feelings or thoughts does the rapid advancement of AI evoke in you? Fear, excitement, indifference? Why do you think you feel this way?

3. Identify Your Mental Shortcuts: Mental shortcuts help us navigate complex

information quickly but can also lead us to overlook important details. Can you identify a recent situation where a mental shortcut might have led to a misunderstanding or missed opportunity?

Embrace Experimentation:

1. Expand Your Cultural Lens: Choose a culture or country different from your own and spend a week immersing yourself in its practices, whether through cuisine, media, literature, or music. Note any new insights or changes in your perceptions regarding this culture.

2. Engage with AI Creatively: Experiment with an AI tool that you haven't used before, such as a language learning app, an AI-based creativity tool, or even a simple AI chatbot. Observe how this interaction affects your view of AI's role in human creativity and productivity.

3. Challenge a Mental Shortcut: Identify a mental shortcut you frequently use and consciously challenge it for a week.

For example, if you tend to make quick judgments based on first impressions, make an effort to learn more about the people you meet before forming an opinion. Reflect on how this changes your interactions and perceptions.

Journaling Prompts:

- After expanding your cultural lens, write about an aspect of the culture that surprised you or changed your previous perception.
- Describe your experience with the new AI tool. Did it enhance your creativity or productivity? How do you envision such tools supporting your future work or hobbies?
- Reflect on the mental shortcut you challenged. Was it difficult to avoid using it? Did challenging it lead to any new discoveries or insights?

These exercises encourage you to step back and examine the frames of reference that guide your understanding of the world.

> By increasing your self-awareness and embracing experimentation, you can see beyond your habitual perspectives, unlocking new possibilities for growth and understanding.

5.
Mindset Zone

While it's crucial to distinguish between the three main approaches to mindset in research to ensure we're comparing apples to apples, in our day-to-day lives, we benefit from a more practical definition of mindset.

Mindset or Mindsets

In fact, I prefer to speak about mindsets in the plural rather than the singular form because it more accurately reflects reality. We don't possess a single, unchanging mindset. Just as research reveals various approaches to studying mindsets, our personal experiences show that we can exhibit both fixed and growth mindsets in different areas of our lives. Moreover, acknowledging the plurality of mindsets opens us up to exploring more possibilities; our minds are not set in stone but are flexible and adaptable.

Practical Definition

My short-hand definition of mindsets comes directly from the etymology or origin of the word[1]: "habits of mind formed by previous experiences."

Yes, we can embrace mindsets as habits of our minds dependent on beliefs, conscious or unconscious, formed from past experiences. And, yet, to grow, we may have to challenge some of these habits, and associated beliefs, what we think we know or even see. We can develop and multiply our potential in many different ways. In addition, understanding our cognitive processes can also help us adapt to new challenges and expand possibilities.

Learning how our brains work to solve tasks and challenges can be incredibly powerful in unlocking our human potential. Learning about habit formation and transformation can help shift our mindsets in resourceful ways.

At the same time, we must acknowledge individual, group, and cultural biases in any given situation. These are frames of reference that work as filters we see through, often without being aware of it. They are like contact lenses or glasses that we forget we wear.

Accelerating Change

This is especially relevant in a world of accelerating change, where norms and expectations often change faster than we can articulate them. For instance, an event organizer publicly recognizes a grant recipient. Her intentions are genuine and heartwarming—she wants to spotlight the generous spirit of that community and the opportunity created for someone who deserves it. Unintentionally, this action triggers feelings of exclusion for this Black woman grant recipient, who doesn't want to be perceived as different from the other participants. This is a real situation I witnessed that was resolved because the grant recipient dared to speak up, the event organizer was open to feedback, and we all learned from the experience.

For starters, I realized the bias in my initial reaction when the grant recipient voiced how uncomfortable she felt with the mention. Internally, I reacted with ageism, "This younger generation has to develop a thicker skin," and felt empathy for the event organizer, "I know how tough it is to be there trying to make everything work, and then...." Yet, when I realized that my past life experiences and unquestioned social conventions were framing my perception, I started to see the bigger picture. This allowed me to understand the experiences of others different than myself, expand my worldview, grow my mindset, and be in awe about the possibilities for our future together.

By leveraging mindsets, you can create transformation. As Donella H. Meadows[2], one of the most influential environmental thinkers of the twentieth century, explains, "These [leverage points] are places within a complex system ... where a small shift in one thing can produce big changes in everything."[3] So, what are the best ways to work on our mindsets?

The Concept of the Mindset Zone

This brings us to the concept of the "mindset zone," a space for exploring and expanding our mindsets. Inspired by Vygotsky's Zone of Proximal Development (ZPD)[4], I've adapted this idea into what I call the Zone of Proximal Growth (ZPG). This concept represents the space just beyond our comfort zones, not so far out as to paralyze us, but just enough to stretch our capabilities and expand our horizons.

A personal adventure into my own Zone of Proximal Growth occurred recently at a professional event in California, where I was invited to try indoor skydiving. Initially, the thought of it was outside my comfort zone. Yet, I asked myself, "What's the worst that can happen?" and I decided to embrace the challenge. The experience was fascinating and joyful, a testament to the power of stepping into the unknown with an open mind and a willingness to experiment.

To have a mindset zone, where we can play with our mindsets or mind habits, is often crucial for us to dare step into our ZPG. Then, magic can happen. With the right support and conditions, we can connect the dots, see things differently, and undergo mindset shifts that enable new solutions and approaches. The ZPG is not about reckless risk-taking but about stepping into new experiences with adequate support and guardrails, ensuring a positive and growth-oriented experience.

Navigating the Mindset Zone

To leverage our mindset zone effectively, we must be mindful of our current mindsets while being open to growth and change. This requires acknowledging our individual, group, and cultural biases and being willing to challenge them when necessary. It's about creating transformation and understanding that a small shift in perspective can lead to significant changes in our lives and the world around us.

Press PAUSE & Sharpen Your Pencil

As we delve into the concept of the Mindset Zone—a safe space to explore and expand our possibilities—it's vital to pause and reflect on our own mind's habits and how they shape our perceptions, reactions, and actions. This section is designed to help you explore your mindsets and encourage you to step into your Zone of Proximal Growth (ZPG).

Increase Your Self-Awareness:

1. Reflect on Your Mindsets: Think about different areas of your life—work, personal growth, relationships, hobbies. Identify where you predominantly hold a fixed mindset and where a growth mindset prevails. What triggers the shift between these mindsets for you?

2. Explore your ZPG: Consider a recent challenge or opportunity that pushed you slightly out of your comfort zone. How did you respond? Did you embrace the challenge, or did you hesitate? Reflect on the thoughts and emotions that influenced your decision.

3. Acknowledge Biases and Filters: Identify a situation where your initial reaction was shaped by a bias or a preconceived notion. How did this perspective influence your behavior? Were you able to recognize and adjust your mindset?

Embrace Experimentation:

1. Step into Your ZPG: Choose an activity or challenge that lies just outside your comfort zone, something you've been hesitant to try. It could be a new skill, a public speaking opportunity, or even a physical activity like the indoor skydiving experience shared earlier. Commit to trying it within the next month.

2. Journal Your Journey: Keep a detailed journal of your experience stepping into your ZPG. Note your initial feelings, the process of facing the challenge, and the outcome. Pay particular attention to any mindset shifts you experience and how they affect your approach to the challenge.

3. Seek Feedback: Share your ZPG experience with a trusted friend, mentor, or coach. Discuss any insights gained and how you might apply these lessons to other areas of your life. Feedback can provide valuable external perspectives that enrich your understanding of your own mindsets.

Journaling Prompts:

- How did stepping into your ZPG challenge your existing mindsets? Were there any surprises?
- In what ways did support or guidance (if any) help you navigate the challenge? How can you incorporate this support into future challenges?
- Reflecting on your ZPG experience, how do you feel about facing similar challenges in the future? Has your mindset shifted in any way?

This exercise is designed to encourage exploration and expansion of your mindsets, fostering growth and adaptability. By consciously stepping into your ZPG and reflecting on the experience, you can begin to see the transformative power of mindset shifts and the potential for personal development that lies just beyond your comfort zone.

PART II

ACTUALIZE YOUR POTENTIAL

In 2014, I started the Mindset Zone podcast to create a space where people could go to expand what they thought was possible for themselves, the people around them, and the world. When my podcast was selected for The Huffington Post's "15 Podcasts That Will Leave You Pondering Life's Big Questions," listed alongside the Peabody Award-winning On Being and TED Radio Hour by NPR, I was on cloud nine. I realized that what I was doing there resonated with others in a significant way. Now, I'm still in awe to see the Mindset Zone ranking in the top half of 1% of more than 3 million podcasts globally!

Yet, life got in the way. Other immediate income-producing projects took priority, and I decided to pause the podcast for a couple of months; it took me more than a couple of years to restart it. That happened in 2021, after lots of tribulations in my personal life, including fighting cancer.

During this journey, I realized that to tap into our human potential, we have to recognize two different types of mindset limitations.

6.
Mindset Limitations - Side A

Beliefs that constrain the way we experience the world around us can be seen as "mindset limitations." These limiting beliefs affect our present reality and impact what we can envision for the future and the possibilities we choose to explore. Often, we are not aware of them. They are mindset blind spots, and as such, they are hidden. Sometimes, others can see them, but we don't. It often takes many painful life circumstances to expose them and give us the impetus to change.

Visual Blind Spots

Visual blind spots are a great metaphor for our mindset limitations. Look at figure 2.

Figure 2: Visual blind spot exercise

Then:

1. Place the image about seven inches away from you (about an open hand away from your nose.)
2. Close your right eye (you can cover it with your right hand.)
3. With your left eye, look crosswise into the minus on the right side.
4. Keep the focus on the minus and notice if something interesting happens to the plus sign.

Sometimes, you have to play with the distance, moving the image away or towards you, but at a certain point, the plus will disappear from your eyesight. Just like magic!

This is where your blind spot is. The area where the optic nerve exits our eye doesn't have light receptors, so we cannot see any images that fall on that spot. If you didn't see the plus disappearing, don't worry. You can google the eye blind spot for more examples later[1]. For now, just pay attention to your inner talk.

So, if everyone has one, why aren't we aware they exist? Well, we usually see with both eyes. One eye sees the information that falls into the other eye's blind spot, and even when we look at something only with one eye, our brain fills in the missing information—our brain tricks us into seeing what is supposed to be there. That's why in Figure 2, instead of the plus that falls into our eye blind spot, we see white space. Our brain gathers what we see from the context around the plus signal and uses it to rebuild what we see.

It's truly awe-inspiring how our brain can fill in the information that's supposed to be there, even when it's not.

Mindset blind spots

In much the same way, our brain tricks us with our mindset blind spots. We believe we see what is really there, but when we have more information, we realize that maybe there is more to take in.

One of my biggest mindset limitations was around my belief that one of the noblest goals in life was to pursue happiness. That was the goal I aspired to and was proud of. I'm an optimist by nature, always trying to see the silver lining in people and life circumstances. I focus on the positive and wholeheartedly embrace the study of positive psychology, speaking about it, teaching it, and even doing a podcast where many of the topics are about cultivating positivity. Only recently did I realize my blind spot around pursuing happiness.

If happiness is a goal, by definition, I'm always pursuing it, and therefore, not enjoying it, not being fully happy. Without knowing it, I had implemented a great strategy to keep detached from my feelings and dissociate from the present moment, which is, ironically, the only place we can experience happiness.

See how that works?

When I started to see my own blind spot, I started to see the possibility of choosing happiness almost every step of the way. Happiness doesn't need to be a goal; it can be a way of being.

Choose to make lemonade out of lemons. Add some sugar (positivity). Enjoy drinking it! Yes, I was making lemonade before, but I did not give myself permission to savor it.

Heroes and Sheroes

I started to understand why I admired people like Victor Frankl, Nelson Mandela, and the kids playing in the ruins of a war-destroyed city. I used to ask myself, how can they smile?

Viktor Frankl[2] survived the concentration camps, where Nazis killed his mother, father, brother, and wife. Afterward, he wrote *Man's Search for Meaning*[3] and created Logotherapy, a form of psychotherapy focused on the search for meaning. Several years ago, I had the opportunity to interview Frankl's grandson, Alexander Vesely, who describes him as funny and witty, with a positive energy that would fill the room. I admire Viktor Frankl's zest for life and his belief in the potential in us all.

Nelson Mandela[4] is another inspiring human being. He spent twenty-seven years in prison fighting apartheid in South Africa. He is known for winning the Nobel Peace Prize and having a fantastic sense of humor.

And my own personal hero, my husband's grandmother, Armen Melikian[5]. Granny lived through the Armenian genocide in 1915—only she and her mother in her family of ten survived the killing and expulsion of the Armenian population from Turkey. She came to the United States in 1923, married, endured the Great Depression with a young son, and became a widow at 49. Only 4'10" in height, full of energy, with a dynamic personality and a biting sense of humor, on her 100th birthday, surrounded by family and friends, she made sure everyone was having a good time.

All these amazing people had such difficult life circumstances, yet they seized every opportunity to enjoy living. How can we learn from them?

Learning Journey

I had to overcome two bouts with cancer to learn that pursuing happiness is a fallacy. In 2016, I was diagnosed with Inflammatory Breast Cancer (IBC), a rare form representing 1 to 5% of all breast cancers, with a 5-year survival rate of 40%[6]. Eight years later, I'm here healthy and strong and have learned a couple of important lessons. Grateful for the advances in medical treatments, I embraced my healing journey with all my strengths. At the time, my mindset was, "I can beat this with all my might, my strength, and my determination." I came to understand first-hand what it is to fight cancer.

I did it. I won the battle.

Two years later, when I was allowing myself to relax and enjoy life again, they found another cancer in my other breast. This time, a more common type that represents 80% of all breast cancers, Invasive Ductal Carcinoma (IDC)[7]. I embraced my healing journey and treatments again, but my mindset had shifted. I realized that feeling betrayed by my body—and going to war against it—wasn't the most effective way to heal.

I decided to embrace my current reality and treat my body like the amazing ally it was to help me get through to the other side.

Perhaps most importantly, I decided to stop the "When… Then…" cycles. No more would

I accept, when I finish this project, then… or when I have more money in the bank, then…. When thoughts like these came up, I reminded myself to live in the present moment and make the most of it—even in the midst of cancer.

For instance, during chemo, I asked to be seated in the treatment chair in front of the window with magnificent views of the Arizona desert.

When all the food tasted like cardboard, I still set the table to enjoy dinners with my family. We even created a ritual of sharing what we are grateful for before we eat. Now, when my 15-year-old daughter's best friend dines with us, my daughter loves to list as many thankfulness items as possible, and that truly makes my heart sing.

Personal and collective traumas like the COVID-19 pandemic awaken so many of us. Those who turn to creativity, nature, and learning—perhaps rediscovering latent talent, journaling, or learning a new language or skill—fare better than others.

Life Circumstances

Life's path is marked by pivotal moments that challenge our established ways of thinking, uncovering mindset limitations and blind spots previously hidden from our view. These instances, particularly during our most challenging times, act as powerful catalysts for deep personal evolution. They compel us to scrutinize our deeply held beliefs and reassess our definitions of happiness, success, and fulfillment.

It's important to acknowledge that while our darkest periods can be profound teachers, the lessons they offer aren't ones we'd necessarily choose or recommend seeking out through similar hardships. For instance, while I've gained invaluable insights through my battles with cancer, it's not an experience I would ever be grateful for or choose for myself or anyone else. My gratitude lies in the medical advancements and medical team that treated me, the unwavering support of my family and friends, and my own resilience and ability to learn and adapt in the face of adversity. Cancer, for me, was not a choice but a challenge thrust upon me. However,

I am thankful for possessing the "mental fitness" and self-leadership to approach my treatment and recovery proactively, allowing me to extract meaningful lessons from circumstances far beyond my control.

This distinction is crucial in understanding the nature of mindset resets. They are not about romanticizing hardship or seeking out suffering for growth's sake but about recognizing and harnessing our innate capacity to adapt, learn, and find strength, even in the most unwelcome of circumstances. It's about acknowledging that while we cannot always control what happens to us, we have a choice in how we respond and what we take from these experiences.

Press PAUSE & Sharpen Your Pencil

As we navigate the complexities of our mindset limitations, it's essential to pause and reflect on the lessons these challenges teach us. This section is designed to help you explore your mindset limitations and encourage you to step into a space of growth and self-discovery.

Increase Your Self-Awareness:

1. Reflect on Challenges: Think back to a particularly challenging period in your life. What mindset limitations did this reveal to you? Were there any beliefs that held you back from seeing solutions or opportunities?

2. Identify Blind Spots: Consider a time when feedback from others highlighted a blind spot in your perception. What was your initial reaction? How did this awareness shift your understanding or approach?

3. Learning from Blind Spots: Reflect on what these blind spots have taught you about yourself, others, and the world.

How has this knowledge influenced your actions or decisions since?

Embrace Experimentation:

1. Challenge a Limiting Belief: Select one limiting belief you've identified and consciously work to challenge it over the next month. For example, if you've discovered a tendency towards a fixed mindset in a particular area, seek out opportunities to cultivate growth through new experiences or learning.

2. Journal Your Journey: Keep a journal of your experiences as you challenge this limiting belief. Note any resistance you feel, as well as moments of insight or breakthrough. How does confronting this belief change your perception of yourself and your capabilities?

3. Seek New Perspectives: Engage in conversations with people who have different viewpoints or experiences. Pay attention to moments when your assumptions are challenged. Reflect on how these interactions broaden

your understanding and contribute to your personal development journey.

Journaling Prompts:

- What was the most surprising thing you learned about yourself while challenging a limiting belief?
- How did seeking new perspectives or experiences influence your mindset?
- In what ways have you grown as a result of confronting your mindset limitations?

These exercises invite you to actively engage with your mindset limitations, transforming challenges into opportunities for growth. By embracing a mindset of curiosity and openness, you can navigate beyond your comfort zone, unlocking new dimensions of your potential.

And, always be gentle with yourself. If something is still too fresh to handle, just allow yourself some grace and time.

7.
Mindset Limitations - Side B

While gaining insights into our mindset blind spots and limiting beliefs—Mindset Limitation-Side A—is very valuable, it's only one dimension of our journey of personal growth. Now, it's the time to put the spotlight on the other side of mindset limitations—Side B—the idea that insights are not enough to create lasting change.

The Influence of Thought on Action

Self-help books, like *The Secret*[1], have popularized the idea that our thoughts are the primary cause of everything. This principle is also the core of many high-performance systems. In one of my favorites, *The 12 Week Year: Get More Done in 12 Weeks Than Others*

Do In 12 Months,[2] Brian P. Moran explicitly argues, "It's important to understand that the results you achieve are a direct byproduct of the action you take. Your actions, in turn, are manifestations of your underlying thinking. Ultimately, it is your thinking that drives your results; it is your thinking that creates your experiences in life."

In sum, most mindset experts see the way we think and the beliefs we have as determining what we do and the results we get.

Cognitive Behavioral Therapy (CBT)

Even the well-researched CBT, Cognitive Behavioral Therapy—a form of talk therapy that has been demonstrated to be effective for a range of problems, including depression, anxiety, and eating disorders—focuses on changing thinking patterns[3].

A classic CBT technique, originally developed by Albert Ellis, is known as the ABC model[4], and it assumes that our beliefs about a specific event affect how we react to that event. This model aims to help us restructure these beliefs and adopt healthier responses.

For instance, you sent an important email out with a proposal that, if accepted, can help you achieve your goals for the next quarter, but one week has passed, and you haven't gotten a reply. This can be seen as the Activation event, the A in this ABC model.

This situation can lead to negative feelings, like anxiety, fear, and lack of confidence, which can result in procrastination or inaction. These emotional responses and behaviors are the Consequences, the C in the ABC model. So, B is at the center of the model and represents the beliefs that are triggered by A and are causing C. The goal is to change the B, the beliefs, or the underlying thoughts. Continuing with our example, when you haven't yet heard back about that proposal, instead of thinking, "How awful! I'm never going to be good at this!"—which will lead to less than optimal feelings and probably a consequent lack of action—you can disrupt the self-fulfilling prophecy by changing your thoughts. This ABC technique can produce great results. Give it a try!

Beyond Linear Change

Thoughts. Feelings. Behaviors. It's tempting to use a linear model to describe what is happening when we are trying to change. Yet, we can argue that this linear perspective is too simplistic and doesn't allow us to see the whole picture. CBT acknowledges that our thoughts, feelings, and behaviors are interconnected, but often, its practitioners focus on changing thinking patterns first, as if our thoughts are the unidirectional cause of our feelings and behaviors. If this were the case, gaining new insights or becoming aware of thought patterns would be enough to change us. Sadly, most of us live with the painful reality that change is not that easy.

Insights Are Not Enough

Wouldn't it be great if an inspiring TED talk was enough to transform us? Yes, it can ignite a spark that leads to change, but usually, there are more moving parts involved in real transformation. Many times, small behaviors can determine the way we think and feel. Consider the dopamine hits we get when we see a "like" on one of our social media posts[5]. We keep looking, waiting to see them add up, continuing the high. We rationalize. We may even say to ourselves, "Likes show that people resonate with my opinion." Or perhaps the likes feed our beliefs, "Someone cares." This is an example of how small actions, in this case, looking at our phones, affect the way we think and the beliefs we have.

Another example would be walking in nature or taking a shower. Doing one of these activities can help us feel more relaxed, more in tune with nature and our bodies, and open our minds to new ideas and possibilities.

The other side of the mindset limitations is that mindset is not the end-all-be-all. Yes, changing our beliefs, our lenses, and the ways we see the world makes a huge difference, yet we need to do more than that. Mindsets have limitations, too. To make things happen, we can tap into the energy that helps us transform and live it through daily actions. And let's not forget the constraints created by social norms and systems.

The Power of Just Exhaling

Sometimes, it's easier to start with small actions, like exhaling fully to the point that we activate the muscles in our belly. Imagine you're a kid determined to blow out all the candles, even the trick variety. The act of fully exhaling has the potential to change the way we feel and think. Give it a try!

Visualizing Change: The Triangle Model

Instead of seeing your thoughts, feelings, and behaviors linearly, I invite you to see them in a triangle. If a triangle loses one of its sides, it ceases to exist. I even invite you to form a triangle with your hands. Your thumbs can connect to form the base of the triangle, the left fingers together can make another side, and the right fingers make the third side, touching each other at the top to form the triangle. Then you can imagine that one side of this triangle represents your thoughts or mindsets, another your feelings or emotions, and the other your actions or behaviors. You can expand a lot of possibilities this way.

Remember the example of the important email still unanswered one week later? That can trigger some anxiety and judgy thoughts towards oneself, "You didn't write a strong enough proposal," or towards others, "How inconsiderate are they?" or even get overgeneralized and impact the way we see the world, "Not fair. This should be easier."

Looking at your triangle, you can start to focus on one action. For instance, by breathing out fully first—go on, blow out those candles—your body can inhale more deeply afterward and with less effort. From that breath, you can see things in front of you in more detail. Colors may even look more vibrant. You remember that stat about the average person receiving more than 100 emails per day[6]. Maybe you decide to send another email, phone, or text to the person confirming that they received your proposal. Why not?

Consider how the insight you got from watching an inspiring TED talk or presentation plays out on every side of the triangle. How will this new way of thinking change your energy, feelings, and actions? What daily habits will you need to practice to make that mindset shift stick? As you move forward, what will you do to sustain the thinking required for the up-leveled way you feel? How can you make this new way of being your default?

Expand What's Possible

This more complex picture provides more entry points for change. Understanding the intricate dance between our thoughts, feelings, and behaviors illuminates the path to meaningful change. While insights into our mindset limitations can be a great starting point, they are not the only way and not alone sufficient for sustaining lasting change. Real growth requires integrating new behaviors and thought patterns into our daily lives in a consistent way. By recognizing the limitations of our mindsets and the interconnectedness of our thoughts, feelings, and actions, we can navigate toward a more fulfilled and authentic existence.

Press PAUSE & Sharpen Your Pencil

Embarking on a journey to transcend mindset limitations demands introspection and a willingness to experiment with new approaches. This section invites you to pause, reflect, and engage in exercises designed to foster a deeper understanding of your mindset dynamics and encourage actionable change.

Increase Your Self-Awareness:

1. Mindset Reflection: Identify a recent situation where you felt stuck or hindered by your mindset. What beliefs contributed to this feeling? How did these beliefs affect your emotions and actions?

2. Insight to Action: Think of an insight you've gained about yourself that you've struggled to translate into change. What practical steps can you take to embody this insight in your daily life?

3. Behavioral Shifts: Reflect on a small behavior you can modify that might influence your mindset positively. How

can this small change impact your feelings and broader perspective?

Embrace Experimentation:

1. Actionable Insights: Choose one insight about your mindset that you wish to act upon. Design a simple, measurable action plan to integrate this insight into your behavior over the next two weeks.

2. Journal Your Progress: Keep a daily journal of your experiences as you implement this action plan. Note any challenges, successes, and observations about how this change affects your mindset and overall well-being.

3. Feedback Loop: Share your action plan and progress with a trusted friend, coach or mentor. Seek their feedback and discuss any adjustments that might enhance your journey toward mindset transformation.

Journaling Prompts:

- How did the process of turning insight into action challenge your existing beliefs?

- What resistance did you encounter, and how did you address it?
- Reflect on the impact of this experiment on your mindset. Have you noticed shifts in how you think, feel, or act?

These exercises aim to bridge the gap between understanding our mindset limitations and implementing tangible changes that reflect our growth aspirations. By actively engaging with our thoughts, feelings, and behaviors, we can craft a more conscious and intentional path forward, one small step at a time.

8.
The P.I.E. Method

We know change is difficult. When the rubber meets the road, it's easier to go back to old patterns of doing, feeling, and thinking. Yet, we can think of our efforts to change as a game where we play and try different options.

To create real transformation, we must understand how our thoughts, feelings, and behaviors interplay and dare to embrace the messiness of the process.

The illusion that change is a linear process and that relapsing into old patterns is a failure is one example of the misunderstood dynamics that prevent real positive change from becoming our new normal.

The P.I.E. Method

To make this journey more enjoyable and playful, I want to introduce you to a simple yet powerful method I teach many of my clients. I also end many of my talks about how to increase our impact without burning out with this practical tool that can be easily learned and remembered, with the acronym P.I.E.—thus, I called it the P.I.E. Method™.

"P" for Pause

Let us start by experiencing the P of the P.I.E. method. Please grab something that you can write with. You can use a pencil and any piece of paper you find near you and write the word "REACTIVE," ideally, all in CAPS: R-E-A-C-T-I-V-E. Now, pause a moment and find the letter "C" between the "A" and the "T." Move that "C" to the beginning of the word. What word do you have now? Yes, you now have the word "creative." You see, you made a small shift that created a big change. A small, simple shift can create a meaningful transformation.

One of the keys to amplifying our impact without burning out is to learn to stop being reactive and stay more in the creative mode.

Another word you can use is proactive. You are not reacting to what happens to you; you are able to respond effectively. You are response-able, and the key is to learn to press Pause—the "P" on the P.I.E. method. "P" is for Pause.

Maybe you are familiar with this quote[1]:

> ***Between stimulus and response, there is a space. In that space is our power to choose our response. In our response lies our growth and our freedom.***

Powerful!

The challenge is to press the pause button after a stimulus triggers us, yet that is what allows us to see the space that gives us the power to choose our response. This is especially difficult to do under tough circumstances.

We need to learn to press this pause button in order to respond to life's challenges without reacting and without falling into old habits. When we do this, we give ourselves the opportunity to be more proactive and respond effectively. And we can train and strengthen the capacity for pressing this pause button as we would do with a muscle. Pauses can be very powerful.

In practical terms, there are three types of pauses:

1. **Macro-pauses**, like working with a coach, listening to an interesting talk or going to a retreat. These can be considered macro-pauses because we create a significant amount of time or space for learning and self-awareness.

2. Another type of pause can be the ones we schedule in our day-to-day, almost like a ritual or habit. This second type of pause I call "**Scheduled pauses**." That morning ritual of planning the day, writing in our journal, or reflecting on our day.

3. Finally, we have the **micro-pauses**. As we become more mentally fit, we can press the pause button by simply being aware of our breath. That can be what we need to create that space after the stimulus that allows us to choose our response, even when we are triggered.

By practicing macro and scheduled pauses, we increase our capacity to do micro-pauses and be able to respond more effectively. Yes, this inner work of self-leadership is like fitness. We have to exercise, but we can find enjoyable ways to develop our mental fitness and become more resilient. This is a way to play in our Mindset Zone and allows us to move to the "I" of the P.I.E. method.

"I" for Increasing Self-Awareness

In the previous chapter, we went deep into how powerful it can be to expand your awareness of your thoughts, feelings, and behaviors not as simple linear causation but as 3 sides of a triangle.

Remember that insights alone are not enough to sustain change. It's essential to practice triangulating thoughts, feelings, and behaviors. For instance, ask yourself how new insights or specific thoughts interact with your feelings and if they inspire action. Expand your self-awareness by considering how changes in your thoughts, feelings, or behaviors affect each other.

We need all these three dimensions—thoughts, feelings, and behaviors—and if we become more self-aware of how they interplay with each other, we can expand our possibilities in a big way.

Which is easier for you to notice? For some people, it would be their thoughts. Others, their feelings, or their actions. For instance, through nurture, I have become a very good neck-up person. I'm very aware of my thoughts and all my mental chatter, including my inner critic voices. I'm also very high in implementation and action. It takes a bit more effort to be aware of how I feel at the moment. I know others who are very much in touch with their feelings, aware of their emotions, and have more challenges in articulating what is going on inside their heads, their thoughts, and belief systems.

If you use our triangle, becoming aware of what is easier for you, is the smarter strategy to use. This is your starting point, and you can always ask yourself how one dimension affects the others. And how you can play and experiment with them.

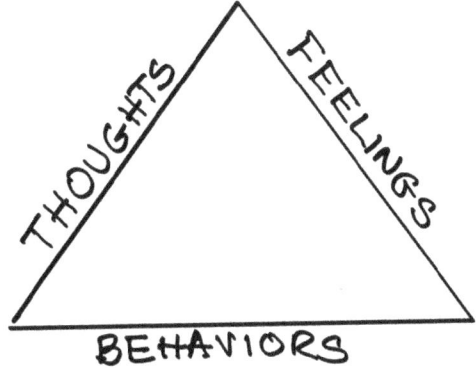

Figure 3: Thoughts-Feelings-Behaviors Triangle

"E" for Embracing Experimentation

When scientists design an experiment, they have expectations for it, and they get surprised and not always happy when those expectations are not met. Yet, some of the most significant advances in science happen as a result of it. In our journey of personal development, it's important to embrace this experimentation mindset, too! Then, all the outcomes are welcome. Well, maybe after some struggling and self-development work. If we don't get an expected result, you can see that as very enlightening. Then, there are no failures, just helpful information to learn from.

For instance, you decide to experiment with creating a scheduled pause to start your workday. Maybe you even save a breathing exercise on your web to practice when you sit in front of your computer. Great! You do it, and you become aware of how that makes you feel. Does it bring more clarity to your day? Does it help you to be more focused? In the next day, you forget to do the scheduled pause.

Please be gentle with yourself. Don't let your inner critic take over. Now you have more information to increase your self-awareness and try again.

My invitation to you is to embrace the messiness that change almost always brings.

In a nutshell, create opportunities to practice pressing pause (P) to Increase your self-awareness (I), and then when you decide what you want to try, you can Experiment with it (E).

This simple method can make all the difference. Just try it.

> "P" for Pause - and we have macro-pauses, scheduled pauses, and micro-pause.

"I" for Increasing our Self-Awareness on how our thoughts, feelings, and behaviors interplay with each other. The triangle.

"E" for Embracing the Experimentation Mindset and playing with it. There are no failures, just helpful information to learn from.

Let's use this simple yet powerful P.I.E. method to unlock our human potential.

Press PAUSE & Sharpen Your Pencil

If you've been engaging with the "Press PAUSE & Sharpen Your Pencil" sections throughout this book, you've already been practicing the P.I.E. Method—perhaps without even realizing it. These exercises are designed not just for reflection but as practical applications of Pausing, Increasing Self-Awareness, and Embracing Experimentation. If you've skimmed through these sections, consider this an invitation to dive deeper. Schedule regular time to revisit and truly engage with these exercises. They're not just tasks; they're opportunities for growth and exploration.

Reflect on Your Journey with P.I.E.:

Look back at your responses to previous "Press PAUSE & Sharpen Your Pencil" sections. Can you identify moments of pause, increased self-awareness, or experimentation? What did you discover about yourself?

Scheduled P.I.E. Time:

Decide on a regular schedule to revisit these exercises. It could be weekly, bi-weekly, or monthly. Mark it on your calendar as your P.I.E. time—a dedicated moment for personal growth and exploration.

Experiment with a New Perspective:

Choose one exercise from a previous chapter that you found challenging or skipped. Approach it this time with the mindset of experimentation. There's no right or wrong, only learning and discovery.

Journal Your P.I.E. Experiences:

Start a P.I.E. journal. After each scheduled session, jot down what you paused to reflect on, any new insights into your thoughts, feelings, and behaviors, and what experiments you're inspired to try. Note the outcomes of these experiments, regardless of whether they met your expectations.

Eat a Daily Slice of P.I.E.:

Integrate the P.I.E. Method into your daily life. Find moments for pressing pause, be mindful of your thoughts, feelings, and actions throughout the day, and treat new experiences as experiments. This could be as simple as taking a deep breath before responding to an email, noticing how certain tasks affect your mood, or trying a new approach to a routine task.

Share Your P.I.E. Insights:

If you're comfortable, share your insights and experiences with a friend, family member, or colleague. Discussing your journey can deepen your understanding and encourage others to explore their own mindset zones.

By actively engaging with the P.I.E. Method, you're not just reading about change; you're embodying it. This method isn't a one-time fix but a continuous practice that can lead to profound personal growth and transformation. So, press pause, sharpen your pencil, and let's dive into the mindset zone together.

9.
Mindset Zone to Actualize Your Potential

It's essential to recognize the need for a safe space to enhance our mental fitness[1]. Just as physical fitness allows us to climb steep stairs without losing our breath, mental fitness empowers us to face life's myriad challenges without succumbing to overwhelm or negative emotions. This inward work is one of the keys to unlocking our human potential.

The Power of Mental Fitness

Mental fitness is not merely about coping; it's about thriving. It's about stepping into each day with a sense of purpose, ready to navigate the complexities of life with grace and agility. It allows us to recover from setbacks with greater speed and resilience, turning obstacles into stepping stones for growth.

A Safe Space for Growth

Creating a safe space for this inner work is paramount. It's in this space that we allow ourselves to pause, to reflect, and to engage deeply with our thoughts, feelings, and behaviors. This sanctuary of self-awareness is where we cultivate the strength to choose our responses, embrace change, and grow beyond our perceived limits.

The Journey of Continuous Learning

Our path to mental fitness and unlocking our potential is a journey of continuous learning. It's a path defined not by a final destination but by the richness of the experiences we gather, the lessons we learn, and the growth we embrace. Each step forward, each challenge met with courage, and each moment of insight adds to the tapestry of our lives, weaving a story of resilience, joy, and boundless potential.

Embracing the Flow of Optimal Performance

The ultimate reward of mental fitness is finding ourselves in the flow of optimal performance—a state where our well-being flourishes, our relationships deepen, and our impact on the world magnifies. This state of flow doesn't need to be a fleeting moment but a way of being, our MO or Modus Operandi, accessible to us as we continue to nurture our mental fitness, challenge our mindsets, and embrace the full spectrum of our human experience. This is even more critical in the midst of the AI disruption and can allow us to harness the power of technology to enhance our humanity.

Expand What's Possible!

As I press pause on this chapter of our shared journey, I'm filled with gratitude. Gratitude for the opportunity to explore this mindset zone together, for the insights shared, and for the collective aspiration to expand possibilities. I like to think of our time together here in this book as if we are children playing in a sandbox, embodying the beginner's mindset and embracing the joy of exploration. Yet, the journey does not end here. Let's keep:

- sharpening our pencils!
- practicing the P.I.E. Method!

- increasing our Mental Fitness!
- and actualizing our human potential!

Go on, expand what's possible!

For you.

For the ones around you.

For the world.

PART III

RESOURCES

Notes

Chapter 1: What's a Mindset?

1. French II, R. P. (2016). The fuzziness of mindsets. *International Journal of Organizational Analysis, 24*, 673-691.

Chapter 2: Beliefs

1. Dweck, C. S. (2012). Mindsets and Human Nature. *American Psychologist, 67*(8), 614-622.

2. Dweck, C. S. (2006). *Mindset: The New Psychology of Success.* New York, NY, US: Random House

3. Eide, B., & Eide, F. (2011). *The Dyslexic Advantage: Unlocking the Hidden Potential of the Dyslexic Brain.* London: Hay House.

4. Lechter, S. L., & Reid, G. S. (2009). *Three Feet from Gold: Turn Your Obstacles Into Opportunities!* Shippensburg, PA: Sound Wisdom; Reprint edition.

5. Carol Dweck's TEDx talk: The Power of Believing That You Can Improve. https://www.ted.com/talks/carol_dweck_the_power_of_believing_that_you_can_improve

Chapter 3: Information-Processing Sets

1. Gollwitzer, P. M. (2012). Mindset Theory of Action Phases. In *Handbook of Theories of Social Psychology, Vol. 1* (pp. 526-545). Thousand Oaks, CA: Sage Publications Ltd.

2. WOOP by Gabriele Oettingen - https://woopmylife.org/

Chapter 4: Frames of Reference

1. ACEC – Association of Corporate Executive Coaches: https://acec-association.org/

Chapter 5: Mindset Zone

1. https://www.etymonline.com/word/mindset

2. https://en.wikipedia.org/wiki/Donella_Meadows

3. Meadows, Donella H., and Diana Wright. Thinking in Systems: a Primer. Chelsea Green Pub., 2008. And also, https://donellameadows.org/archives/leverage-points-places-to-intervene-in-a-system/

Chapter 6: Mindset Limitations - Side A

1. A great resource for understanding our visual blind spot is https://faculty.washington.edu/chudler/chvision.html

2. Bushkin, Hanan, et al. "Searching for Meaning in Chaos: Viktor Frankl's Story." *Europe's Journal of Psychology, vol. 17*, no. 3, 2021, pp. 233–42.

3. Frankl, V. E. (1959/2006). *Man's Search for Meaning*. Boston: Beacon Press.

4. https://en.wikipedia.org/wiki/Nelson_Mandela
5. https://www.legacy.com/us/obituaries/azcentral/name/armenouhi-melikian-obituary?id=26040210
6. https://www.cancer.org/cancer/breast-cancer/about/types-of-breast-cancer/inflammatory-breast-cancer.html
7. https://www.hopkinsmedicine.org/health/conditions-and-diseases/breast-cancer/invasive-ductal-carcinoma-idc

Chapter 7: Mindset Limitations - Side B

1. Rhonda, B. (2006). *The Secret*. New York: Atria Books; Beyond Words Pub
2. Moran, B., & Lennington, M. (2013). *The 12 Week Year: Get More Done in 12 Weeks Than Others Do in 12 Months*. New Jersey: Wiley.
3. Beck, A. T. (2005). The Current State of Cognitive Therapy: A 40-Year Retrospective. *Archives of General Psychiatry, 62(9)*, 953-959.
4. Ellis, A. (1995). *Better, Deeper, and More Enduring Brief Therapy: The Rational Emotive Behavior Therapy Approach*. New York: Brunner/Mazel.
5. Dopamine & Social Media Addiction:

    Macit, H. B., Macit, G., & Gungor, O. (2018). Research on Social Media Addiction and Dopamine Driven Feedback. *Journal of Mehmet Akif Ersoy*

University Economics and Administrative Sciences Faculty, 5(3), 882-897.

https://sitn.hms.harvard.edu/flash/2018/dopamine-smartphones-battle-time/

https://www.iomcworld.org/open-access/neurotransmitter-dopamine-da-and-its-role-in-the-development-of-social-media-addiction-59222.html

6. https://www.cityam.com/inbox-anxiety-how-regain-control-email/

Chapter 8: The P.I.E. Method

1. For the origins of this quote, read QI - Quote Investigator article: https://quoteinvestigator.com/2018/02/18/response/

Chapter 9: Embrace Mental Fitness to Actualize Your Potential

1. I credit the work of Shirzad Chamine, and his "Positive Intelligence" program for introducing me to the concept of mental fitness.

Acknowledgements

Writing this book has been a journey of exploration, growth, and profound gratitude. It's a path I haven't walked alone, surrounded by the support, wisdom, and encouragement of many incredible individuals. This section is a small token of my appreciation for the collective contribution that has made this book possible.

First, I want to extend my heartfelt thanks to Katie Peuvrelle, Irma Jennings, and Mary B. Simon. Your insightful feedback on the initial version of this manuscript was invaluable, inspiring me to refine my thoughts and persevere. Your encouragement was a beacon of light on this journey.

A special acknowledgment goes to Clementina Esposito, who taught me that a writer does not write alone. Clementina, you have been instrumental in helping me translate my spoken voice into the written word, a gift for which I am eternally grateful.

Marie Kaye, your belief in my ability to turn my content into a full-fledged book has been a source of strength.

To my coaches and mentors—Mitch Axelrod, Greg S. Reid, and CB Bowman—each of you has left an indelible mark on my journey. Mitch, you helped me realize how close I was to the finish line when I needed it most. Greg, your inspiration to think bigger has expanded my horizons. CB, your courage and example have been a guiding light.

To my clients, who inspire me every day with your growth, challenges, and triumphs. A special thanks to Kari Wick, who keeps asking for more Mindset Zone content.

To my family, who are the bedrock of my existence. Jim, my husband, your unwavering support has been my anchor. Bella, my daughter, you inspire me to grow every day. To my incredible sisters-in-law, Mona and Nevine, and the entire Melikian and Hye family, your support knows no bounds. To my mom, brother, and niece back in Portugal, your presence and love span the distance between us.

Lastly, to the Mindset Zone podcast reviewers, followers, and listeners—your engagement and feedback have been the wind beneath my wings. Your stories, questions, and insights have shaped this journey in ways I could never have imagined.

If I have inadvertently omitted anyone, please know it was not intentional. My gratitude extends far beyond the confines of this page. We are all continuously learning, and there is always something to be grateful for. Thank you, from the bottom of my heart, for being part of this journey.

Thank you for reading!

If this book has sparked new insights, inspired change, or offered you valuable tools for navigating the complexities of life and work, please consider leaving a review on Amazon.com or GoodReads.com. Your feedback not only supports me as an author but also helps other readers discover the transformative potential of this work.

Moreover, if you know someone who could benefit from the insights and strategies discussed in this book, I encourage you to spread the word. Whether you pass along your copy or gift a new one, you're contributing to a ripple effect of positive change and growth.

Free GIFTS for YOU!

The journey of exploration and growth never truly ends; it continually unfolds, revealing new paths and opportunities.

Discover free gifts and resources by scanning the QR code below.

Scan this code to unlock resources that complement the ideas and practices shared in this book.

About the Author

Ana Melikian, Ph.D., is an international speaker, author, and host of the MINDSET ZONE, which ranks among the top 1% of podcasts worldwide. Ana's mission is to empower purpose-driven leaders and organizations to increase impact and results while avoiding burnout, overextension, and disengagement.

A survivor of two bouts of cancer, Ana embodies resilience and champions change through effective self-leadership. Her journey is a testament to the power of overcoming adversity and leveraging personal challenges as catalysts for growth and transformation.

Recognized on the *LeadersHum PowerList* 2023 for her contributions to unlocking human potential, Dr. Melikian is also a *Board Certified Coach* (BCC) and an active member of the *Association of Corporate Executive*

Coaches (ACEC) and the *National Speakers Association - Arizona* (NSA-AZ).

Before moving to the US, Ana taught at various universities in Portugal and Spain and co-authored several scholarly articles and book chapters. She earned her Ph.D. in Psychology from the University of Sunderland, UK, laying a solid foundation for her work that integrates research data with practical applications in psychology and coaching.

Currently, Dr. Melikian is at the forefront of exploring Humane AI. Her work aims to harness the power of artificial intelligence to augment human potential, ensuring that technological advancements enhance, rather than diminish, our humanity and collective well-being.

www.ingramcontent.com/pod-product-compliance
Lightning Source LLC
Chambersburg PA
CBHW031403160426
43196CB00007B/873